HEALING TO MY FEELINGS

SMRUTI PATEL

Copyright © Smruti Patel
All Rights Reserved.

Healings to my feelings

Smruti Patel is a passionate writer and her debut book Healings To My Feelings is a poetry book that allows us all to walk through every feeling we experience in our lives. She likes scribbling in her journal and she's also a songwriter.

For more updates, you can follow her on instgram (@smruti_2254) or mail her at patelsmruti492@gmail.com

Contents

Acknowledgements   *ix*

Prologue   *xi*

1. Clover   1

2. Moon And Serenity   5

3. Imagination   8

4. I Miss You   10

5. Dear Miss Taylor   12

6. Driving Back To Nashville   15

7. Shattered Flowers   18

8. The Ring   20

9. Vintage Cottage   22

10. I Wish We Were Meant To Be Together   24

11. The Realization   27

12. Heal Again   30

13. Writing A Song   32

14. Lavender Blossoms   34

15. Folklore And Quarantine   37

16. I Could Close My Eyes   39

17. Sinking Ships   41

18. Back For Holidays   45

19. Dear Cell Phone   47

20. Season Of Fall   49

Contents

21. What Lies — 55

22. Where Do You Go? — 57

23. What It's Like To Be A Therapist — 59

24. In The Aftermath — 61

25. Abandoned — 64

26. Like A Flower — 67

27. Bluebird — 70

28. It Takes Time To Grow — 73

29. Healings To My Feelings — 75

30. A Phase When I Was Alone — 77

31. Just Me And Her — 79

32. Man — 83

33. Diary — 85

34. She lost him but Found Herself — 87

35. Mama's Lullaby — 90

36. Forlorn — 92

37. I Know — 94

38. Over The Creeks — 96

39. 15 Seconds — 99

40. Wisteria — 100

41. When An Aquarius Loves — 103

42. Looking Back At You — 106

43. 18 — 108

44. The Best Place — 112

Contents

45. Blue 114

—

About The Author

Acknowledgements

I'd like to express my deepest thanks to Taylor Swift and other songwriters and writers out there for always being my inspiration, and for the way, they keep inspiring me to create art; I would've never written anything if their words weren't standing by my side.

I would like to pay my special regards to my parents, of course, some of the beautiful readers that I made, through this journey, who always are so inquisitive, and the way they've just supported me, I can't thank you enough. Lastly, I'm thankful to all of you.

Prologue

The reason I felt I needed to start writing…

I always wanted to write, since I was a child, I thought that someday I would be capable of writing things that are hitting my mind now and then. But I didn't have enough words to stand up for the way I was feeling. My mind was like that of a juvenile, not that mature. Slowly and gradually I started growing up and so did my mind.

I realized that I didn't have that many friends nor did I show any interest in outdoor and indoor activities or sports, I sensed I was so lonely, so I used to study like a well-behaved one, I had lost the hope that there was nothing around me that can give me consensus or serenity. And there's just one thing left for me to do: go stand in a semblance of the mirror, recite whatever comes from my mind, and carry it to my tongue.

Years enacted and I turned 18, Well, it's a long story short that we all know, how 2020 became a very pathetic year in everyone's life, each of us was completely broken, tiptoeing back and forth. The virus was coercing us very badly. We were whirling so protective towards our family members to protect them from the trap of COVID, We were second-guessing what if it took away the person we care about the ones we love the most. I was pointed up too, so I decided to find a way out of this rabbit hole and that's how my journey as a writer and writing begins.

Initially, I used to write about the way I was thinking or how everything is going on. How I turned into an adult too fast. When I started writing I didn't have that many words nor a very well-fitted adjective, or vocabulary, my brain was still busy analyzing whatever I possibly thought for. But I decided to just give it a shot and at this point, I want to thank Taylor Swift for always being my moral support unknowingly though she wasn't with me still she was with me, her words, were always standing by me her lyrics, were running hover me I use to see her convey very important messages during her music interviews to all the young generation out there creating art, to all the creative songwriters, vocalist, guitarist, that 'Never stop giving up on writing, own the work you do, be proud of it no matter how bad or good it is because that's the only way artists grow and battle against their demons, changes they are facing in their lives, defeating their enemies and that hit me hard.

From that day ahead, I also tied a notch in my head that I'll write to. I won't give up. Though I'm not good at it now, someday I will be. Then I started writing about various things, like imagining stuff from different angles, sifting it differently, and putting my ingenuity into words, rhymes, and melodies. And then I started writing it on paper, I started looking for various words on the internet as time enacted.

By the end of three months, I wrote my first poem, called 'Clover'. Then after the time limitations of nine months, I started writing my songs and I still couldn't believe the fact that this is the feeling that I had felt, my perspective, my idea, my melodies, my choruses, my verses, etc that I've written. But it came out so intrinsically in a very startling way that I could've never imagined. After a while, I reached that level that I almost wrote my first two albums at the very same time.

They were all inspired by the fiction I read when I was still processing to write. It played a very important role, to make my songs look and shaping them more beautiful and realistic. I put myself into the character's shoes and thought what if this happens then it would end up in this habit. I started looking for various standpoints and then creating my own stories, naming characters, metaphorizing the lyrics and so much more.

I started waking up at midnight if something sticks in my head and then sitting on my couch and completing writing fast as soon as I forget it, and write till dusk. I've always been such a fan of country music, God damn it they're such phenomenal storytellers. There are so many female artists like Loretta Lynn, Carly Pearce, Deana carter, Kelsea Ballerini, Dolly Parton, Dixie Chicks, Shania Twain, Miranda Lambert, Trisha Yearwood, Reba McEntire, Vonda Shephard, Colbie Caillat, Carrie Underwood, Mariah Carey, little big town, Lady antebellum they are infinite. Like they have always been my inspiration.

And now that here I am ready to put down all my poems on pages, I'm ready to put my feelings in words and rhymes, for which I've poured my heart, my body, and soul into every possible way, and everything that I could've envied for. All the poems are about different feelings where we are feeling, the way we are denounced, the way we are broken, scathing, happy, confused, lonely, overlooking our bygone days.

Writing for me has now become a very substantial part of my life and my escapism from this sunken world. Now I feel if there's no writing there's no me. I'm so fastened to writing's gravity and magnetism, that even if I try to stay apart I can't help ignoring writing poems and songs anymore. I am conveying all these various stories from my life that I came across starting back from my childhood till now. So it's time to wrap yourself in a cozy blanket, grab a glass of wine, and my book it's time to relax y'all, it's time for you too to feel it, letting it all go, cause there are always healings to everyone's feelings.

- Smruti Patel

1. Clover

I think when I was seven at a time,
And never knew life stains color like wine,
Sometimes I rewind how I cried,
Summers pass and rains come by,
I just remember all the good times,
Being a youth sure has its ups and downs,
It seems I'm learning something new each time I turn around,
Things are modified now for me than when I was young,
I'm older now and wiser too and life's a lot more than fun,
Tied to duty and my studies,
So I take a little way off from this busy life and take a visit to my hometown,
To clear my head, and push aside all the worries
Where I'm unrestricted to do my thing, slow down and smell the roses
I used to think when I'll get old the fun would be all over,
I'd sit by the rocks and dream about bygone days near the clover,
Days of fun and frolic that were filled with love and fun,
Wide fields to run,
Just drinking lemonade,
Laughing all the streets when I pass home,
No worries short stories at bedtime,

My mom used to be with me all night,

Back when,

My dad used to tell me 'I was his little brave sword',

And he use to let me drive his black Ford,

Someday I miss being myself on my own,

Making friends and playing guitar sitting by the school stairs,

So I just let me down in Clover,

Just myself enjoy without no lover,

There I'll set my soul free,

To bask in memories of my youth,

When life was carefree,

Where ambitions of pixies still hover,

Watching the bees and butterflies in

beautiful summer skies,

Let me smell the color green,

It feels just so cool,

Let all the freshness,

Heal all my wounds on my working skin,

When I look at the four-leaf Clover,

It reminds me of what all life has been,

Sometimes fun,

Sometimes like sinking ships,

Returning to the place and time,

Where I grew up committing impish crimes,

Where integrity remains to discover left laughter,

In accidental themes,

Even bitter chocolate has a better taste,

I lay in Clover,
There I'll rest my weary and tired bones,
Upon the soothing leaves back and forth,
Where my childhood fiction was drizzled,
Back when I and my friends used to play in the Heather fields
under the silver moon,
Done from studies and French stories,
Just go and make wreaths of flowers and stone jewelry,
And watch the spring bloom,
Don't know where life takes me,
There are so many stairs till you climb the stakes,
So I just sit in the field and discover peace of mind,
And Clover you're the heal that makes me feel myself find,
So I let myself for a while in Clover,
Where I'll let myself anxiety-free,
Where the green confetti of nature showers its blessings upon
me,
And bring me back to my childhood memories,
I let the smell of green soak into me,
And this is the place where my childhood grew in Clover
fields,
From spring to summer,
Summer to rains,
Rains to autumn,
Autumn's to winter,
Till the time Clover redden again and again.

- Smruti Patel

2. Moon and serenity

Well, we were there then,

Saturday night and with a deep conversation all began,

Just me and her upon the roof,

I have a good pal and she gives me hope,

We only get a weekend to talk,

So we don't squander time at all,

We are the species of girls living in a world where we collide

with people who extort,

At least we have each other and a vacant seat,

We were talking about a life filled with dollars,

She said "she wants a good life and job that is white-collar",

I know she's haggling with a lot these days,

Some phenomena that arose in her way,

We were gossiping shit about boys,
But everyone we look for looks more like a toy,
Don't know where life will carry us,
But we hope for a fairer place that won't hurt,
I told her to relax and just let it all go,
Because autumn is the season when we all collapse and grow,
Yeah, we may sound outrageous but we speak the fact,
We cackled, we kidded, and exhilarate ourselves,
We want a life with red wine and a good compilation of books editions on our bookshelf,
Well, life is not what we expect,
That's what detectives like us suspect,
Just two girls conserving dreadful secrets,
It was not only just the two of us but the calmness in the atmosphere,
But also the moon concealment in the clouds who was listening to our talks from our back,
We strived and asked the moon,
Please find us a promising date very soon,
We don't want to spend our whole life being a wallflower,
So please your highness stipend our wish before we become old,
But not when we will have ruffles and we won't look like gold,
She was talking about her wish to have her own company, the moon whispered back to 'calm down honey,
it's not easy as it looks to make a lot of money,
Wish we had a place like a moon to count on so that we could

drift away like a butterfly

And that was the night just the two of us upon the canopy,

Praying for the possibility,

Praying for existence,

Two secluded chicks under the pale moonlight,

Well, there was nothing but the moon and serenity by our side.

- Smruti Patel

3. Imagination

I'm not someone's expectation,
But I am a good soul called imagination,
If people hold me I am the reason for their happiness,
And if not then I'm simply a delusion,
But anyways people feel happy with my illusion,
I am sometimes a rainbow for people in their darkest days,
Sometimes flower for people who are in love in their way,
I can be something crazy,
If people imagine summers
They will find me hot and lazy,
I am never with someone but still, I can bring them a smile,
I'm a good soul called imagination in their life files,
The world is colorless without my existence,
I am the reason people survive in the worst condition,
I'm chocolate to girls who had a breakup,
Sometimes lipstick for girls who can't survive without makeup,
I'm not someone's expectation,
But I am a good soul called imagination,
I don't like people who don't care about me,
They will see me like a nightmare in their wildest dreams,
But I don't like to hurt someone,
Because when they are lonely I bring a grin to their face,

I like the way I play my ace,

Take control over everyone's mind,

But there is no place where I can hide,

The world won't be happy without me,

So I just dig in everyone's sleep,

They get lost in a wonderland,

To a place full of daydreams and snow lands,

Because I'm not someone's expectation,

I'm a beautiful soul called imagination.

- Smruti Patel

4. I miss you

I'm trying to move on, I'm trying to be my own,
But it doesn't make me feel happy,
Days are flipping so fast look at me still feeling sleepy,
I don't know why?
Yesterday I tried to write a new chapter,
Can't help but again, I got lost in that letter,
That you gave me last time,
When you were mine,
When will I feel normal again?
It's becoming tough to escape this pain,
When I turn on the tv,
I watch that same movie that you used to watch with me,
I strive to step on different steps,
But it hauls me back to you...
Can we take out the smoke, Can we breathe in the air,
Would you like to come back to me I guess it's not that late,
I am sorry that we both got hurt,
I'm here to confess to you, that I miss you so much,
I woke up this morning dreaming about you,
Even when I don't think of you,
Is it my subconscious mind that can get you out of my sight,
I don't know what it's like to feel alright,
Cause your glimpse ride like a roller -coaster,

Look at me I'm never growing older,

Every time I try to read a new chapter,

But how can I stop myself from getting lost in your letter,

God, they all are still close to my heart,

Why past always has to hurt so much

Try to step out still searching for your eyes,

I feel like a trapped butterfly without you even if I can fly,

It's fading outside,

And I wish you were here,

It's getting colder,

And I wish your warmth was here,

I know love is the worst fiction,

Didn't know when you became my addiction,

If I told you we can drive that same old road again,

If you reach early by tomorrow we still have a chance to begin,

Would you like to come back to me I guess it's not that late,

I swear this time we won't hurt each other

I'm here to confess to you, that I miss you so much.

- Smruti Patel

5. Dear Miss Taylor

Dear Miss Taylor,
I grew up too fast, I love the song
Tim Mcgraw from your past,
You might have some champagne pulled off that shelf,
Your songs are full of mystery and I love them to solve,
I ain't thought I could ever write songs,
Your words were like an alarm that gave me the nerve to write
something so long,
I wonder it must be cool to write songs about guys who cheat,
Breakups that happen and won't let you sleep,
But you were prepared to stand strong, even if it cuts deep,
You're a long way from Nashville,
Grew up in Pennsylvania raised on a Christmas tree farm,
When I listen to you I don't feel disarmed

Dear Miss Taylor...
The song picture to burn was the first song I played,
Back when I was sixteen to a boy who didn't even know my
name,
And reputation was cool with the song called end game,
Life keeps rolling all the time,
At least I have you and you're songs with mine,

Even in the worst breakup, you taught us to never go out of
style,
Take a little break cause you're been working for a while,
And cardigan became the hit song,
Some lyrics that no one could write,
I wish someday I would come to visit Tennessee,
And get a chance to sing with you at the bluebird and have
one glass of whiskey,

Dear Miss Taylor,
We both grew up too fast,
And wish you could tell me, how do you make everything last,
I ain't a good songwriter,
But I'll always try,
You're the reason I love country music more than the sky,
I ain't a good songwriter,
But I've been a beginner,
And I heard the truth,
And I can feel your pain,
Now I know why you sang 'all too well' that way,
Yeah, I know why you sang it that way,
You taught me so many things before I realized it was in me,
You brought a lifeboat in me sailing back on the tides,
Now writing to me makes me feel like a ride,
I can feel those tears in your hush,
It's normal to take a break from all this rush,

I can't imagine a day without listening to you,
I find something in me new when I'm with you,
Don't know where life takes you,
But I hope for a better place and better time,
You had everything for a while...

Dear Miss Taylor,
There is least I can do,
I have you where I can go,
A lifetime of the story was a few years long,
You run in my mind and thoughts when I do something wrong,
Thankfulness is the last word that I have in my dictionary,
Or else no words have been discovered to greet you,
I'm only me when I listen to you.

- Smruti Patel

6. Driving back to Nashville

It's been three years and a half since I left my hometown,
Settling in California and still don't know how to turn things
around,
Guess that's the reason I'm dancin' round and round,
Fell in love with a boy,
He thinks he can break my heart as if it were a toy,
All-day job and work no time to enjoy,
So I just packed my stuff
And grab my car keys,
Put on my belt and pull the backseat,
And drive southside,
I know a place where I can rest my feet,
Feels like all the whiskey gone wrong,
He was so mean so I just couldn't stand with him for so long,
My mama's waiting for me,
I need her side and let myself free,
I got a reason to go,
So I'm driving back to Nashville
I finally reach home,
Hug my mamma and held her tight, I cried a lot like it hasn't
rained for a while,
It's been a few years since I haven't talked to her,

My teen days weren't that blur,

My front porch reminds me of my friends,

Days I spent with them writing songs and nights that never
used to end,

There's a picture of me in my bedroom when I was three,

I recall it all back when my life was beautiful and carefree,

I don't know how I grew up too fast,

Was it my fault if he didn't make us last,

So I just grab my car keys and drive Highway 101,

I found a place for me where I can fly,

I spent a few months drowning in tears,

So I just gotta a reason here,

Yeah, I'm driving on the county roads to forget it all,

So I'm driving back to Nashville,

I sleep with the hope, maybe tomorrow will be better,

And I don't want any scarlet letter,

Cause being with my mom and my town sounds better,

I know sometimes whiskey goes wrong,

So to turn it right I've traveled this way along,

I need a break from all of this

I know a place exactly where I can hit,

So I just grab my car keys,

Put on my belt and pull my backseat,

I need a break from all this,

There's a place where I can hit,

And drive southside,

I know a place where I can hide,

So I'm driving back to Nashville
To forget it all.

- Smruti Patel

7. Shattered flowers

As we broke up we drive our separate routes,

I don't have a reason to wear high heels, so I wear normal shoes,

I sit in my home, don't know how to overlook,

All the colors are fading into a faint view

Looks like did you ever love me?

Like the way I did,

So all I do now is sit by the window and see all the green and yellow meadows,

Remember where we use to lay our heads,

All the roses are turning colorless,

Do you even recall me when you drive in that car?

Why did you leave me alone trapped in that jar,

I was so optimistic when you were with me

my life looked similar to movies,

Guess it's all lost in the midways,

Roads have now shut down to reach your heart-way,

No breath left in me,

I am not a rose, I am like shattered flowers tumbling alone,

All your memories won't let me sleep,

And all I have is your vintage cardigan to keep,

Nightmare shows up again and again,

Now I don't want to give you any chance to begin,

I remember the night you gave me that ring,
How easily did you get a chance to swing,
All I do is walk around,
Your past is all over me can't feel the ground,
I know when you were with me,
I had more beautiful sunsets to see,
Now I'm dying alone in the bedroom looking at your ghosts
and how they look at me...
Guess it's all lost in the midways,
roads have now shut down to reach your heart-way,
I am not daisy,
I am like shattered flowers receding alone,
I am not a rose, I am like shattered flowers,
that can't be healed anymore,
Hope that it's all over for good,
I spend my days walking in the woods,
Telling myself that,
Wish someday I'll be a rose,
I don't want somebody who likes to choose,
I hope for a love who will love me the way I am,
Guess it's all lost in the midways,
Roads have now shut down to reach your heart-way,
No breath left in me,
I am not a rose,
I am like shattered flowers collapsing alone.
- Smruti Patel

8. The ring

Long handwritten letters lying in my closet,
Words how little they mean but I keep them in my pocket,
Keep the lamp turned off hang with a bottle of wine,
Good girls like me don't know how to feel fine,
I'm reading the page where our storyline ends,
Is there a place in this world where I can stand?
I feel like an idiot for loving you,
All you did was paint those walls gray instead of blue,
Try to step out, but it's hard
Try to forget you, but it hurts
One moment gave me the ring,
the second moment you called off our thing,
everything was good when you were mine,
Packed your stuff and left for L.A,
And I spend my days with no one's arm to lay,
Guess you have found someone new,
Loved me and gave that ring to someone I don't even know,
When did your loving heart begin to look like a stone,
When did all our memories start breaking into pieces,
My new dress is made up of scars,
Once it did shine like stars,
Try to weep, it's getting dark,
Try to wake up, I am no more a lark

One moment gave me the ring,

the second moment you called off our things,

everything was good when you were mine,

Wish things between us would've been better,

Now I'm nothing but a Scarlet letter,

Was I so bad, that you have to leave my side,

Can someone tell me the best place to hide?

Everything was good when you were mine

When you were mine.

- Smruti Patel

9. Vintage Cottage

I'm depleted of this life that I have,

I'm tired of sauntering on these same pave,

I'm tired of illustrating to people who I am,

I'm left with nothing but a stain,

Where my life is nothing but pain,

I want to evade these miseries,

To a place full of daffodils and yellow roses,

A place where I can hide,

I'm nauseous from all these car rides,

A place where the birds chirp and perch on the branch,

To a niche full of birch land,

I know a vintage cottage,

Hiding deep inside the forest,

Where everything's just right,

The window blooms with wisteria and lavender,

And the dusk set's in candlelight,

The oak trees growing taller than my hope,

Sometimes you're fastened when you need a rope,

To clean yourself from this mess,

And lay your head without any stress,

The windows dance in ivy and the cottage is underwritten with woods,

A place where everything is good,

A small gate that opens the door where I can find happiness,

The dawn awakes with melodies of bees and butterflies,

A place I won't feel apprehensive,

I want a cottage life,

I'm done being a good wife,

Guess I know a place,

Deep inside the forest,

Where the brooks flow calmly like brooks,

Where no one cares how I look,

So I'm fleeing this life and escaping this place,

To a vintage cottage to hide my face.

- Smruti Patel

10. I wish we were meant to be together

Two years back and it all started,

I fell to the ground for the first time I saw him,

I did everything to keep his notes in my pocket,

But the second moment I got to know,

That he has someone more than me, she's naive,

she's fine then why does he stare into my eyes all the time,

He pretends like it's nothing,

Feels like I'm stuck in between the scenes,

Yes she's beautiful but not pretty, does she make you feel special or petty?

Tell me boy what's wrong with you,

it's me, after all, why can't you see it through,

I thought I should burn it over if you and I aren't together,

but a part of me needs you

I wish we were meant to be together.

So I tried hard to block you from my way,

But I failed because your flashback started bothering me in every way,

Years later we meet again,

I try not to look at you,

you were standing feet apart from me in the mall,

I wish if you ever tried to call,

But it never worked the way I wanted,
All these pictures of you in my mind leave me haunted,
I see you stand by her makes me feel like shit,
Why don't you just end it?

wish we were meant to be together,
It might help me feel better,
How easily I was caught up by the moment that I almost
sensed that you smell like a rose to me,
but when I tried to wrap myself around you I could feel all
the stings,
I think it's so easy to mess up with your feelings,
Why don't you come back to me and heal it,
I would grab all the pain from you,
I'll take that as my pills if it helps you to sleep at night,
It's been a while,
I'll be turning 19 this year and so will you,
wish If we were together we would blow the candles,
or maybe that's what you don't want I would hold you till
midnight,
Guess it'll always remain a dream of mine,
Cause I knew from the beginning girls like me don't have a
reason to shine,
I'll blow the candles alone,
I'll save a wish for you keep mine aside,
Wish if we were meant together It would've been alright,
And it was my waste of time, but why did you always make

me feel like you were mine?

That's my story,

I've smoked a lot without a pack,

Lost myself, now how to get it back

I wish if we were meant to be together,

It might help me sleep better.

- Smruti Patel

11. The realization

The realization.

So I sat on the bench, in the middle of nowhere, resting my hand on the other,
I felt peace as it prevails around me,
When there was no respite, listening to James Taylor, through my earphones,
I had my journal with me so I took it out and I held it close to my chest, as if I was holding an infant in my hand, and grabbed my pen so tight as if it was the only mountain remaining to save me from the fall,
I wrote and wrote, till my lungs and heart emptied every single note it had buried for so long,
I lost myself somewhere where it becomes difficult to come back from, something more analogous to my home.

Still, Making an effort to figure it out...

Laying my head on the bedroom floor sessile with the cessation that bloats in my room, 3:AM at midnight pacing, crying, laughing, tossing, twisting, thinking about nothing, acting ferociously, and stank.

-A little confused me.

Why abandon your beauty, wearing makeup, when you can look so pretty with those freckles, little brown spots on your skin giving sea-shore vibes, why straighten your hair when you can flaunt in your curls, which symbolizes that you're perfect with your every single imperfection, beauty never lies in pretending, it lies in honesty, God has shaped all of us with different details, then why all of us is too busy acting so frail?
- To the reader.

Everything I see around me is tangible,
But why does it feel that it is fictitious,
They say it's very lenient to understand what a book wants to convey,
But when it comes to reality, no one knows what to say,
At last, we go and linger around the escarpment or a precipice,
Or sit by the table watch the candle reduce into a complete mess,
We investigate it so carefully till there's no hope that it can spread light again,

Furthermore, we can not be everything they want us to be,

Once the candle melts it can't be converted into a new one

from the same amount of wax,

Everything is pretty confusing, isn't it?

But we're helpless,

Clueless, concealed

Everyone has to incline before time,

Just go with the sequence and just try to work things better,

That's the trivial every one of us can do,

Rather than giving up on life,

And die dead,

Because nothing is normal as it appears,

And nothing is simple as it glimpses,

But I can persuade you that it is not as easy as it looks.

- Smruti Patel

12. Heal again

How easily you believe someone when they lie,
How easily they mess up with you and make you cry,
You don't see what's there on the other side of the door,
Later on, you realize you're the one who's lying on the floor,
You let the door open for them to walk,
They leave you broken like chalk,
My new bookmark is designed with trust issues,
My tears won't dry even if I weep them with tissues,
But you broke me in the worst way,
There's complete darkness I need some sun rays,
You left me wounded, I don't know from where to begin,
I don't think I'm gonna heal again,
It takes some time to grow,
It's not like you'll feel better by tomorrow,
A butterfly lurks through my window,
Takes all my pain and flies over the meadow,
Tells me to let it go,
Soon autumn will get over and it'll snow,
My new bookmark is designed with no issues,
My tears will dry soon I don't have to wipe them with tissues,
I'm feeling better in a good way,
Darkness is fading slowly I can feel the sun's rays,
You left me wounded, but I found a way to begin,

I feel soon I'm gonna heal again,

I sense I'm gonna heal again,

That butterfly taught me something I didn't expect,

Don't let people in, this is what I suspect,

They'll try to show you all their concern,

The second moment they'll make you forget what you had learned,

It's time now to leave it all behind,

I don't want something to take control of my mind,

I've broken so many times,

But that butterfly made me convinced that it'll be alright,

It hurts a lot to be wounded,

No sooner someone comes and heals you again,

Soon all the flowers will dance,

Life will always give you a chance,

You'll break sometimes you'll forget from where to begin,

But someday, all your pain will heal again.

- Smruti Patel

13. Writing a song

It's captivating to see and feel how something trickles out of your mind like emanating brooks,

When you're reluctant of reading letters,

You need to do something to make yourself feel better,

And that's when you snatch a paper and pen that's completely lifeless until you let all your feelings set free,

Then a seed starts to thrive and broaden its roots reaching your mind,

Soon it starts to develop and grows into sectors of thought,

A leaflet of stance comes out whacking,

Slowly and slowly leaves of words stack and align,

And a bud of ideas gets ready and blooms into a flower of phrases,

All the flower petals alleviate on the paper that it almost gives it life,

Then word by word,

Rhyme by rhyme,

Chorus after chorus,

A song is born,

When you feel so happy even if it is way too long,

You can express it in anyways you want,

So take a bottle of wine,

Take your journals, maybe your guitar or piano and start

putting your thoughts into something realistic,
But don't stop writing until it lowers your weight,
That's how it feels like,
Writing a song...

- My escapism,
- Smruti Patel

14. Lavender blossoms

The blossoms of lavender and the Mediterranean sea,
Nothing elegant like that
I have ever seen,
Flowers all shaded in purple and pink,
I guess what's that color violet or lilac?
The fragrance of equilibrium and peace it spreads,
Feels like we are clenched to nature with petals of lavender like
it's a thread,
The sun's rays scatter its lustrous reflection,
A place that dances in different colors and affection,
The flower that rises in its way,

Reminds me of my childhood days,

Back when I used to create wreaths and stone jewelry,

But now life is not at all the same then I expect,

I see the colors that remind me of something,

Loves a scabrous hallway and when someone becomes your everything,

Fragrant tiny buds,

potent enough to soothe the atmosphere,

I get lost when I see these lavender blooms where every moment seems straight and nothing's at all like a sphere,

Purple lavender,

Grows in a large open field,

The field smells so good,

Reminds me of South Carolina and bluebell Virginia,

Wish when I will get stale,

When I won't look fierce,

When my skin will turn pale,

Wrinkles will show up and when I'll start to waft,

I'll come here and reside between these lavender blossoms and see my beauty with it,

And make some lavender wreaths to put in my hair,

And remember that life isn't fair,

You always get what you deserve,

And there's nothing continual that you can preserve,

I like the way the lavender blooms,

Bold and fearless,

It glows perpetually and never feels restless,

And there's so much I can say about the lavender blooms,
It always gleams while others gloom.

• 36 •

- Smruti Patel

15. Folklore and quarantine

I just can't get over with it, it wouldn't be fun if you couldn't
be 'The one',
And then I felt like I was an old 'Cardigan' under my bed, and
I just wanted to visit 'The lakes', but then,
I was awakening from an 'Epiphany' and singing 'Betty' all
day,
And wanted to party but sadly
I couldn't because there was no 'Mirrorball',
And the whole damn year was like 'This is me trying' and my
mind was in 'Exile'
And heartbreak got me to feel like,' my tears ricochet', And
everything was 'Hoax',
I didn't get 'peace', and reading novels reflecting 'Illicit affairs'
became my job for the whole day,
And 'August' slipped away like a bottle of wine and no one
was mine,
And staying home for a year made me a 'Mad woman' and
when
Writing became my 'Invisible string',
I learned good things about Rebekah Harkness from 'The last
great American dynasty'
And that's how I spent my quarantine days with folklore.

- Smruti Patel

16. I could close my eyes

How does someone pretend to be good at a time?
That once seems green, but then cloaked in yellow,
Laying my head under a calm and green willow,
But suddenly comes a dark cloud,
And you dropped my hand when the atmosphere, started yelling loud,
I scoured for your side but you disappeared,
I think of a world where elation lies,
Wish I could close my eyes, and quest myself,
Back where he left me behind like a catalog on a shelf,
How someone can showcase to be so kind,
One moment together, the second moment it's hard to get him out of my mind,
Just like the color violet,
Break my heart with words that aren't polite,
Picturing myself in thorns,
Once seemed roses and now that it's becoming a threat,
I don't know how to get through,
I believed in you because even your false was true,
Cause the songs that you played for me didn't have any chorus and interlude,
How was I so silly that I didn't see the side of you that was rude,

Sometimes they say it's good to let it go,

But it's heavy to clasp it back,

Wish I could close my eyes and search for happiness,

But everything is broken down and there is sadness,

Wish I could close my eyes and I wish I never saw you,

I was so wrong that you weren't the person that I knew,

People like me get hurt every time and that's nothing new,

Wish I could close my eyes, and

And waft away,

To a place where I don't have to suppress my fears whether it's

day or night.

- Smruti Patel

17. Sinking ships

Your gentle side feels so good next to mine,
And sometimes I think about us late at night,
And I don't know why?
I wanna be somewhere just you and me,
I wanna be where you are with me,
But you're there,
I'm here, hurling pebbles in the river,
You and I Fell hard, and hurt ourselves
I didn't see the waves coming,
And you left my hand when we started running,
And I'm sitting on the front porch,
I lurk my anxieties so I could help you to trade yours
I didn't mind getting spare scars if it meant healing yours,
Now I am the one who's lying on the base,
And we both are drowning down like sinking ships.

- Smruti Patel

—

It's time to say goodbye,

this is the last time I'm saying hi, I'm sorry I did maim you, I'm
sorry couldn't love you, I'm letting you go, you'll find someone
more.

- Smruti Patel

18. Back for holidays

It has initiated snowing again,
All the snow tumbling like my wishes,
And all the white confetti,
Coating the ground
I can see the hustle outside prowling through this windshield glass,
And I'm waiting for time to pass,
When you'll come back to this town,
To lay our heads down upon the roof,
Like we always used to do,
And visit the lakes,
It's the season of love and hope that has come back again,
I'm waiting with wide eyes open just waiting for you to walk in,
But the times ticking,
And I'm descant,
I'm blushing more than all these Christmas roses, chrysanthemums, and ivy,
It's been a year since you left,
I'm finally getting the nerve to drift,
And kiss under the mistletoe,
With my eyes closed, there's nothing I want more than you for this Christmas,

I've put on your favorite dress,

I still look pretty in my lilac chiffon and my hair looks better
even if it's like a mess,

I've decorated the Christmas tree putting each decor as my
will,

For you to come back this time,

And the porch is glistening with the Christmas lights,

The mailbox is overloaded with Christmas cards and letters,

All I want is you to come back to our town

back for holidays,

I hope when I'll wake up the next morning,

I wish to see your face.

- Smruti Patel

19. Dear cell phone

Dear cell phone, I wonder what my day would be without you,

I wonder if I mess up with someone, how can I stitch things again without you?

When I'm broken I have your shade to come and cry under it,

You're always there to heal me,

Anyways, you wear a beautiful wallpaper that is covered in lime,

My days start with you and end with you,

I don't know why people consider you as non-living,

When you are enough to understand the way I'm feeling,

You work as a band-aid to my wound,

You heal my broken heart,

And don't let me know that I'm back to normal,

You carry all the hatred that I pour on you,

But I want to apologize for being so rude,

Though I didn't mean to hurt you,

You understand me more than anyone else,

My body goes numb without your pulse,

I don't know how to thank you,

But the problem is my parents don't like you much,

Because they think you cause me a distraction,

But I'm helpless because I can't resist your attraction,

I've learned so many things from you,
I've learned to write songs and poems with you,
You correct me when I show up in errors,
You always listen to my talks even if it's way too long,
Dear cell phone thank you for tolerating me every time,
I cannot find someone honest like you even if I try,
You're always there to wipe my tears when I cry,
Dear cell phone without you my heart breaks in two,
But please don't leave cause I don't have a place elsewhere if
there's no you...

-It's really hard to survive without you

- Smruti Patel

20. Season of fall

The leaves have started withering again,

Just like a heartbroken person with a broken mosaic heart,

Everything is swirling into pieces,

And I miss all our clandestine kisses,

This season prompts me of you,

All the autumn colors make me cold-blooded,

I sit inside my room like I'm burrowed,

I see all the lovers passing the streets,

Guess I'm not cause I don't have your coat around my arms to

keep me warm,
It's still hard to believe that you ended,
The flashback from our rememberings however keeps me surrounded,
But the conflict is now I'm grounded,
Everyone is sitting on the bench,
I feel so lonely and now I'm heading to visit the ranch,
I remember our walks and talks on the pavement,
You were my greatest achievement,
That still reminds me of how good you were to me back then,
And my life is misery as you go,
It's so difficult for me to tolerate all this,
Autumn's come every time and seal my doom,
Don't you remember back when you used to give me faith?
I see people delighted,
But for me, nothing's straight and easy,
I'm so drunk all over these feelings,
Is there any season for my healing?
I wish if autumn never came,
And everything would be alright,
But destiny takes you to places that are never straight,
All I can do is hope for better,
And I'm still living in fallacies waiting for your letter,
The season of fall comes and goes,
That's the story of a life where sometimes you don't play it cool,
So I sit in my bed and nudge the season of fall till the springs

bloom again,
And when my life will commence.

- Smruti Patel

—

Let me find escapism from the world, when your shadow is not around to pick me up when I am about to fall, let me find someplace for me to go and cry, I need a little escapism to step in light, step in daylight.

Nothing goes the way you want.

- Smruti Patel

21. What lies

I woke up with a nightmare today,
I saw you fade away from my sight,
It's day outside but I'm not pretty sure that I feel the sun's rays,
Well, I discern the flowers are flourishing but in my psyche,
it's still midnight,
Cause you pretend that you're ok when you're not,
But it's only you who knows what lies beyond the cascade,
I shed some of my tears cause I feel upset about the fact no
one wants me in their life,
When someone asks me hey, how you are I reply to them with
a smile,
Even though I've been feeling so fucked up for a while,
Well, the birds are piping outside,
Honestly, if you ask me I'm so damaged inside,
Cause you pretend that you're ok when you're not,
But it's only you who knows what lies beyond the cascade,
It's only you who knows what lies beyond that smile, is an
ocean of tears,
It's only you who knows what lies beyond that happiness, is
that poisoned ivy of toxicity that grows in your mind,
It's only you who knows what lies beyond that pretending, is
broken, mosaic heart,
It's only you who knows what lies after all.

- Smruti Patel

22. Where do you go?

Where do you go? When for the first time you failed,
You go into yourself and plan to be a better rendition of yourself next time,
Where do you go? When you fall without looking where to fall,
You get cognizant by this time to see twice before you crawl,
Where do you go? When someone maims you with dishonesty,
You will try not to trust someone that easily,
Where do you go? When you had to say goodbye to your best friend,
You'll try to write letters to her and do whatever to keep her close,
Where do you go? When your world diagonals upside down,
You go and cry in your mom's arm which gives you the faith and warmth you need,
Where do you go? When you feel alone,
You'll isolate yourself in your room rather than trying to place all your pieces into this cynical and distorted world,
Where do you go? When one of your friends tries to be mean to you,
You'll try to drive as long as you forget about them,
Where do you go? When you lose the person who was close

to you is no more,

You'll hold on to their memories,

Where do you go, When you throw yourself into someone, the one you love the most, the one without that person you are half dead, splits you out from their life,

You're broken, you're half dead, you lose your reflection, you lose the reason to take breathe,

You don't have anywhere to go, you're fucked up, you're shattered, you're sobbing,

Where do you go? When you're left heartbroken on a lonely path all alone,

Where do you go?

- Smruti Patel

23. What it's like to be a therapist

Hi,
It's me your therapist,
And that's not my story like everyone thinks,
I get up early in the morning and get ready to hear
every person,
Whom I don't even know,
Neither they know me,
I keep the entrances open so that people can come
and share their anxieties and catastrophes with me,
I hear a lot of them,
People who visit leave with acknowledgments to all of
their doubts,
No one cares about the queries I have,
Everyone presumes that nothing is going on in my life,
That's the reason I'm here to guide,
My life apart from being a therapist is a lot more,
More scribbled and despicable than I pretend,
The worst stories in which I've been into that image,
I've been someone's ex,
I've broken so many times,
And so have I gathered,
There are times when I can't even sleep at dark,

I don't have anyone with me who will eavesdrop on all
of the stupid dialogues that I want to recount,
At last, it's me who has to oversee whatever comes in
my way,
I feel what if I had someone who gave attention to me
whatever I want to articulate,
What if I had someone who would toast me when I
come back home with a drowsy face,
But sadly all such things look glorious only in fiction,
Not in reality,
And guess that's my life being a therapist.

- Smruti Patel

24. In the aftermath

It would be incredible today 'I notified myself'

I could make out the perfect smell of Daisy and chrysanthemum in the cinch as I opened up all the windows,

just before I didn't know what was lingering for me,

Here's my tale,

I woke up earlier this morning,

Enlighten by the sickness to see him after so long,

Well it was just weeks 'I mocked at myself'

But my heart answered back as if I didn't saw him for the past few years,

I rise from my cozy bed and walk my feet to the bathroom,

And try to get ready, because no one wants to be late right?

I could make out the smell of elation that was lingering around me,

Not the actual to be reliable,

But from my body that was so engaged analyzing and thinking about him,

I leave my hair undone,

Cause they look more beautiful when they are open just like my mind,

I go nearer to the closet and run my finger through each dress,

But no sooner

I pick up a pink chiffon dress,

Which goes corresponds with my wedge heels,
But as it is said that there is a complete hush before a storm arrives,
Tardily that day I realized that line was meant for me,
I reached there, I could almost feel the bubbles bursting in my belly,
But the next second moment it wasn't trickling,
It was a bit of panic,
When I saw him kissing someone else,
He looked at me but he didn't unnerve to come and say something,
And the same moment he texts me that 'we're done...
I started running from that place,
All the mascara starts to flow down on my cheeks blended with my tears,
See nothing goes like the way you want,
It halted me so badly,
That I could sense the bad smell of smoke around me,
I wish I would have never worn that dress,
I'm a girl who is now looking like complete chaos,
Returning empty-handed except for the weight of thorns and barbs carrying in her heart,
It's an awful feeling to get betrayed by a person,
Who you love the most,
Who you care about the most,
But they are the ones who always make you believe in,
And just because of that you pin yourself into their skin,

And the next day it won't take them long to swindle you,

They will cut you till there's no you,

I'm now living remorse,

My new fashion is pain,

My new life looks like a hoax,

And my new dress is made without stitches,

Because there are no needles with me that can patch things

back in their place,

I gave every inch of my soul to heal his vacancy,

I didn't even notice the way I got stung,

I decided to take all his wounds so he could live in peace,

The only thing I expected was him to be at my side,

I have no idea what to do,

I have no idea where to go,

The last thing I have is me in the aftermath...

Did I ask something more than he can give,

The only thing I asked from him was a perfect ending,

And I'm half-dead,

And that's what life looks like in the aftermath...

-The breaking...

- Smruti Patel

25. Abandoned

What a beautiful life isn't it?
Just staring at the nightlight and sky shoved with stars
together,
A cozy cloak of love dressed around our arms,
Late-night talks about commitments upon the roof,
Your side by mine gives me faith,
And suddenly we tilt upside down
Then comes a phase when everything is fallen,
We are breaking down like parcels of the mirror,
All the oaths you made now seem a hoax to me,
No one has no one's side,
And I don't know what is ethical?
All I am left with is your flashbacks and wraiths,
And pass me alone through gray woods,
No one's there to patch my lacerated heart,
You have gone away, far from my sight,
One awful fight,
And I'm left in the consequence at night,
I didn't look when I was about to fall,
I knew that despite everything I'll crawl,
So one moment you called it to love the second we
called it quits,
I'm an abandoned sky over the emerald seas,

What a romantic book?
Where we inscribed all the stories with the ink of belief,
Then comes the rain and turns it to rust,
And how our story starts to lose all the lust,
The pages have started drenching in the lakes of trust
issues,
And no anchor around to save us from the fallout,
None of us is left with anything,
All we do is go our separate ways,
I see all the barbed wires that envelop my talon,
I'd rather take hate than love,
Cause I don't know how to handle it like it's okay,
This is how you feel when you're accused,
So one moment you called it trust,
The second moment we called it over,
I'm an abandoned sky over the emerald seas,
A windshield window no one could see,
The line pulls apart us in the wrongest way,
None of us know what to
say,
Everything slipped away like a bottle of wine,
I guess it never felt like you were ever mine,
Tricking smiles, heartbreaking things,
Never inferred such broken scenes,
I'm an abandoned sky over the emerald seas,
I'm sobbing but no one to see,
I'm an abandoned sky,

Over these emerald seas...

- Smruti Patel

• 66 •

26. Like a flower

What a delightful creation of Nature,

Made from beads of affection and jewels of care,

A woman just like a flower makes the earth scour its garland and wreath

Her heart is one in million,

Her soul is bigger than the oceans and seas,

But even after so much forbearance and hate,

Don't know how does she feel alive,

She's that petal that retains its sangfroid even when it withers,

Let the weather be drizzle or moisture,
The way she always glows,
The way she flows,
She manages every wave whether it's high or low,
Though the growing lethal roots of discomfort in her,
Her life is full of blows and twinges,
She never lets a plant go burnt,
Her touch is of Midas that can turn dust to gold,
She's that boat sailing for decades and decades crossing all the
sea lines,
All the ups and downs,
Living in haunted and wicked towns,
That is filled with resentment,
And her dress is nothing but scars,
Everyone tries to smash her wings,
When she starts to fly,
Is there someone to stop her fall and cry?
Her perfume is like musk that erases the unpleasant smell of
smoke,
Her hands are like tendrils that grow to aid everyone's life,
Then why does she have to always soak the words that cut her
like a knife?
Her eyes are the clouds that leak,
Rain of love and ceases away the drought of hate and
loneliness,
Her hair symbolizes freedom and ideas,
Her lips are enough to stand the world,

Cause she's like a flower and she'll always be a flower,

But don't let the floods carry her away,

And make her break to the bones,

Just grow that flower the way it wants to, sprinkle some water

of trust and support,

And then see it bloom,

Women are like a flower,

That withers, fall, break, but still beautify the place,

At last, I don't have much to say,

Don't ever try to pluck that smile from her face.

- Smruti Patel

27. Bluebird

Guess I penned a song today,
Finally to get over you, Which I was thinking about it since
prior few days,
It has everything I want to say,
The lyrics enunciate the way you were with me,
The melodies give an account of the way you weren't,
The chorus recounts the heartbreak anthem,
And the bridge interpreting the way I lost myself into you,
And that's how the ballad speaks the story of us,
I call it "It's raining instead of snow",
Do you remember me?
I grumbled in my head,
The very first day you saw me blushing in red,
Now I'm striding back and forth laying in my bed,
Recalling our preface, back when
I saw you at the bluebird cafe on the very first day,
From where our verse
begins,
And currently, everything is different but your recalls still
block my mind again and again,
It feels like I'm foundered,
Can you tell me how to forget about you so easily?
Is there a potion that can help me?

Or a chance to pick up the mess that you created?
The way I looked into your blue eyes while strumming through my guitar,
How do you think, I'm dealing,
I'm solving the quandaries of my mosaic heart to find recoveries,
I guess there's no one by my side interested in seeing the way I am feeling,
I still keep getting by heart the way we wandered in Centennial Park,
Hustle the county roads till highway 101,
Dance around and round near the street under the pale moonlight,
I looked at you like you were the only one to make me smile,
It was just a fiction that made me fall,
Deep into the waters from where I cannot come back,
Now that it's completely chasing,
I'm going through these days inscribing songs,
About the way our storyline ends,
But a part of me still keeps scouring for the footnotes in the story of your life,
Cause now you have some more beautiful than me,
I strive she won't be me,
The one you love,
Then hate,
Pretend it's love and then fake,
So here I am now ready in my cowboy boots and violet scarf

and my hair undone,

Looking at the sun with an urge if it can stitch me again,

Holding my Gibson Guitar,

Heading my toes again at the bluebird cafe,

To tell a story about the way love damages you,

Just to fetch me back,

From the same place where I misplaced it last time.

- Smruti Patel

28. It takes time to grow

I plowed some seeds last year in my backyard,
When I was four,
Years upheld and I've finally learned now how to run the aisles,
But I still wonder how much time it takes to grow?
Summers pass, then rain, then autumn's and last till it's back to normal again,
But the trip is very interesting,
A seed starts to germinate expands its roots and wands itself low into the ground,
Then slowly tiny leaflets start to grow around,
It takes patience to unfold,
but no sooner than the branches are formed,
And then after they are decorated with the green-colored leaves,
A flower bud pops out and imperils itself to the sun as soon as the sunlight falls on it,
And it blooms forever even if the seasons take a drift,
But they always lift,
I discerned them so carefully,
To learn how to grow,
Cause it's not like you sow a seed and it grows,
By tomorrow,

The rate of reaction is very slow,
That's what I have come to know,
So it's not like we can turn in everything we want to be, by tomorrow,
It takes years and years,
Efforts by efforts,
To stand there,
There'll be obstacles, There'll be storms and downpours,
It'll be harsh sometimes to overcome this in vain,
But there'll be hope, out of this mess,
And that's a lesson I've learned from a plant,
That it takes time to grow.

-A journey from seed to a flower,

- Smruti Patel

29. Healings to my feelings

Is it always have to be the way I think,

And at last, it's me holding myself before I shrink,

Can I just have one drink,

Before I cause flings in my brain and heart again,

It's weird, right?

How handily we keep our doors available,

So that every time someone can stroll in whenever they wish,

But we are unknown which one causes the most ravage,

And then we are there again, drowning, tossing, twisting, turning, flickering,

Wishing this would've never happened,

Crying that crazy out of you,

Or shoot tequila straight,

And then we do anything to make ourselves feel good,

Because even after all these discomforts we know this wasn't the climax,

So we rise again and again even if we know we're going to shed down like the leaves in the fall,

But a day will come when we'll be surviving tall,

All we need is to keep history in the past,

Or else no matter how hard you try you'll turn out last,

It's arduous to wake up with the same thought every day,

Where we feel like nothing going to be straight,

There are so many county roads to cross,

Till we enter the highway,

Enjoy every zest of fruits whether it's of disappointment,

sadness, darkness till you figure out that you put the sweetest

apple of happiness in your mouth,

Don't let failure wound you,

Don't let anxiety ruin you,

Don't let fear hold you,

Don't let hurts hurt you,

Cause at the end it is you who's growing stronger,

After tolerating so many acid rains and pesticides,

And now as for me,

I've started putting my steps on these roads,

I don't know how depleted I will be till I'm strong enough,

To carry these loads,

I see everything around supposing it'll be easy,

But it's not,

All I can say is there's a yacht sailing in me,

And my heart confiding my stories,

There'll always be healings to my feelings.

- Healings to my feelings
- Smruti Patel

30. A phase when I was alone

Life isn't decent as I used to think,
I realized when I lost my sight and everything started to sink,
Never knew a pill could change everything,
It was the worst time when I felt I lost everything,
My world wobbled upside down,
And when all my choices were disseminated,
It's the worst scene when you have eyes to see,
Despite that, you can't see,
What life wants to show,
The only thing left in you is to stride with your skull hung low
How can I pick up this mess?
When I can't even see how I look in my little black dress,
How was I allowed to know what was coming,
Just like a bullet shot that eradicated everything that came
into my life when I started achieving,
I was completely broken and shattered into sections,
There was a time when I had seen towering dreams from these
eyes,
But the second moment it went wrong with all my wishes,
The wind took away all my fair dreams, flowers, and trees that
I had grown on the roads,
How can I live with this load,

When,

I was crushed,

I was breathless,

I was scathing,

But inner walls made me realize you can't let go like this,

I wanted to cry that crazy out of me,

But I was left with not a single drop of tear to shed,

How can I even cry,

So I just woke up from this nightmare,

And decided to try,

It was the dullness that had taught me by this time,

What my visions are to me,

So do whatever you want before it's too late or when you won't
live to see,

Be that firefly in the darkest night,

Find your wings and get ready to fly,

I've grown robust and better now,

This was the discourse I learned from a phase of my life when
I was alone.

- Smruti Patel

31. Just me and her

From where should I embark, when and where we begin,
How we were two aliens living feet apart on the firefly lane,
I saw you smoking and scathing like a shattered mirrorball,
So the next morning I ran into you with some handmade marmalade,
That's when our storylines up in a way,
You use to visit my horse anyways,
Back when for the very first time we hope the school bus,
We ran towards the open fields like there was no one like us,
And how we lost ourselves in talks,
And visiting those bushes in autumn,
Dancing and singing under that lamellate early winter leaves-shedding trees,
And set our minds free,
Forthwith nothing is as it was,
Ever since I lost you, my half soul,
And my heart now always bowl,
It was some huge squall that took you away from me,
You were always there for me when I needed you,
And jewels like you are very few,
Now that you visit the doors of heaven,
And for you everything is new,
We were so strenuous to answer every question in brief,

You left me alone just so I can die in grief,

Halloween was always supposed to be leisure,

To dress like one of those hipsters,

I'll always miss daydreaming with you forever,

And now it's barely me,

But there was something more clandestine,

Back when it was just me and her,

We both grew up into grown-ups walking the one-sided firefly lane,

And the way we were all over the streams,

When I was with you I never felt shame,

As I do now,

How would you know it somehow?

Cause you're too busy talking bullshit with those angels, instead of prevailing with me,

You're too industrious with your concerts and karaoke nights,

You used to howl at me when I did nothing right,

How we adorned the Christmas tree during holidays,

Do you remember how drunk we were that night at the prom?

Monday's and Tuesday's busy reading novels that had covers of witches and ghosts on them,

My fingertips don't sense your veins anymore,

We are that separated butterflies,

Wandering two ends but, now belonging to different worlds,

One above,

The other is below,

One is full,

The other is hollow,

I know when I go back to your mom's house every new year,

I think of you standing with me nearer,

Just two sweet-sour girls,

Living and chasing their dreams

I miss being me,

I am only me when I am with you,

Back when it was just me and her,

I hope you'll be somewhere safe and sound out there in this world,

We played guitar together sitting by the school stairs, and sing our favorite song called 'Goodbye Earl',

It was all in our past back when it was just me and her,

I've kept every scrap of you,

That reminds me of you,

And when I used to be pissed off,

You drew me those unicorns and hearts in the by-line,

And made me feel fine,

We were the craziest always out of line,

Watching the crescent golden moon,

Like we never wanted to grow up,

And pretend forever like a child,

I theorize it must be fun,

Turning twenty-nine,

Except it's a clashing phase,

You without me in our picture frame,

I guess no one's there anymore to patch up my tapestry,

When I shed,

Nothing but the cruelty of time,

I wish you were with me,

Back then when it was just me and her.

- Smruti Patel

32. Man

Where did that little boy from that story of his childhood
page disappear,
And started writing new anecdotes,
When did that innocent face,
Change into a nicer and wiser person,
When did that little kid's shoulder widen,
To carry this many responsibilities,
In between, he went through different twists and turns,
Somehow he made him strong to survive all these swirls,
He came out as the better version of himself,
Who started arranging different novels on his life shelf,
When did that smile get more adorable and flawless,
Life isn't fair every time,
And so ain't it's cruel,
But the worst thing is the time and situation,
Nothing else,
I realize now that's the reason, you are so tall,
Maybe to fight all the thorns coming in your way,
Must be missing the fun you had during your bygone days,
But here's to new beginnings,
Turning 24 is a whole lot to feel and say,
But one thing is forever, please stay the same,
Don't ever criticize yourself,

Because you look more handsome with tension,
Your smile looks more flawless when the smile behind the
smile isn't a smile, it's pain,
Don't you ever try to call yourself imperfect,
Because it is the imperfectness that makes you, you,
Hope all of your hurts will heal again,
And don't get devastated because the game has just begun,
When did that person from a little boy upheaval into a grown-
up,
Overnight turned into a man.

- Smruti Patel

33. Diary

Inside a little heart of her, she saves all her memories of old childhood,
Laughter dealt with siblings, a smile on their faces, and walking school with charts and files,
A scribbled chunk of paper written utterances and doodles, and her vintage diary,
Clasping on to the jewels of her missing well-lived life, print in her diary
A long story short of innocence still growing into a grown-up,
Inside the brine of her mind, floats the spirals about the chronology of her days at high school, and detachments that always happened even though he tried in vain, Studying, completing homework coffee at late night,
Thinking about stories with an exact fairytale ending,
But time starts awakening and makes her realize,
'Its time to write her own story,
Where she is never dwindling,
Where she's the star,
And the winner of the war,
She danced with every comet,
Wishing for a world where accomplishment lies,
She was a trapped butterfly longing to be set free and fly,
And then the day came when she meets herself and she flew

away

To a land of greener meadows and white lilacs

Where her wings could finally comfort

A hope, a will, the strength of childhood,

keeping her alive,

This is how it feels, as she grows greener and more elegant

Inside this little locket called her heart she keeps all her rememberings in the vintage violet diary,

Although her childhood has slipped away like yesterday's hail,

But the lifeboat in her always sail,

She keeps each memory inside her pocket that never makes her worry,

All fire, sorry, and secrets buried,

Some from traumas and some from pals,

And keep it secret to the grave and the end,

And silently walk the pavement,

Stepping into the phase of life where nothing's good,

But still precious to her,

And that's the story of how she grew up writing and conversing with her diary.

- Smruti Patel

34. She lost him but found herself

When she fell, she fell hard,

Wrecked her bones and now that ash covering the pavement,

Once she was adorned with kisses and her muse,

And she was deluded by him like she was of no use,

Comfort that she gave, roads that she cleared,

What was her expectation?

Just for him to be near,

She walked the gloomy roads, and troubled forest,

Searching for a reason for the way she was relinquished,
All the footings show its disastrous and scabrous surface,
The way she lost her reflection and face,
She was left with nothing but injury and smudges all over her
dress,
She was still adorable though she looked like a mess,
Left with nothing but broken fractions of memory,
And everything now turning into her furries,
She walked despite the gravel in her alley,
She wept and shouted why she couldn't make things last,
But was it her fault?
No, but still the burden was on her,
Will she find someone someday who'll take good care of her?
She realized she needed to stand
To a place where she's alone on that land,
So, she quivered her maimed wings and tried to fly,
Over the tall oak trees
up to the top of the highest of mountains,
Her eyes still glance,
All that persists in her soul
She lets go of her head,
To start new inception and merge in the ocean of happiness
and escapism,
She lands in a garden where no one will ever hurt her,
Somewhere where the butterflies roam
In the garden,
In the weeds,

Bury all the deep dark deeds,

All that remains is a bony outline of something that makes her,

She feels the drifting breeze

In the upshot, only echoes remain and a seed of hope,

The door sways gently,

The writing on the wall and flashback vanishes,

Wallpaper ruptures from the past,

And when she's finally clean,

She puts her first step to a place that will never dim,

When her inner voice made her realize,

She lost him but found herself.

- Smruti Patel

35. Mama's Lullaby

Let me take you to the spot and time,

Back when I was a newborn when my face looked spherical,

I used to shriek every day and night,

The reason was nothing but the baby heart in me,

Just demanding things that aren't good for me,

Tears used to drip down from my cheeks,

Not a big deal but still forms a slender creek,

Creeks filled with my tears,

When a patron comes nearer and takes my tense,

She takes me in her hands,

The warmth of her flicker makes me feel good,

She tells me a story about a nymph residing in the woods,

My verdant immature brain couldn't know much,

But still, her story always sticks close to my heart,

Suddenly then she sings a melody that is so dulcet,

It felt like a Nightingale is performing a concert,

And an American Robin playing guitar,

The voice was so calm like a serenade,

And now that I've grown up,

There are phases when I still can't snooze,

But my mom the Nightingale she comes again,

And sings a melody and a midway to my sleep begins,

She tells me sweetheart sleep well,

Always rise even when you fall,

Her lectures always give me faith,

So she mutters in my lazy ears,

Wake up early in the morning so you won't be late,

Cause the journey of life is so long till you find the gate,

And that's how I'm strewn with my mama's lullaby,

It's never childish even when you grow up,

It brings a light to my soul day and night,

She's my wings when I need to reach the heights.

- Smruti Patel

36. Forlorn

Forlorn is a quite small word, isn't it?
But guess who knows this word better than me,
It's like being 18 and still hiding in your room,
It's like growing without growing up,
I look around at my friends they look so happy,
Days are passing by, but everything around me looks so dizzy,
People around you have reasons to snuck,
Look at me I'm still stuck,
I tried hard to make a place in the world,
Just so again I get caught up in the same old swirl,
When nobody lets you in,
How can you feel clean,
One of your dreams remains barren,
That you build out when you were a kid,
Being forlorn makes you sick,
Situations are so tough, I'm still confused about which one should I pick,
So you take your phone in your hand,
That's the only place where you can land,
A part of me needs a naked truth,
And someone to tell you 'just keep swimming '
Everyone wants to be Ryle Kincaid,
But no one chooses to be Atlas Corrigan,

You hold on to this treacherous string reading all the books,

Cause nobody cares about your looks,

Maybe you aren't the prom queen,

You're just one of me,

Looking at the flowers reminds me,

Were they ever conceived for me?

Cause I never received one of them,

And the worst part is to see your crush on one of your school friends,

God, he doesn't know I screwed up over my studies just so I could write a song about him,

At last, I don't have much to say,

Except that this world is so mean,

They tell you to be clean,

But how could you hold on when you have no one's side to lean on,

For others forlorn is a noun,

The only word that makes me squeamish when I turn around.

- Smruti Patel

37. I know

I know this was the awful thing I did in my life,
But how was I so stupid to be a knife?
I hew the ribbons of what we had,
And when I came back to my senses,
I could see what I lost it back,
Just rewinding the memories of your pinch,
That's the thing I miss so much,
Would you mind talking with me in brief,
Cause not being with you is my massive grief,
Maybe if you want, I could've given you a chance,
Be there with me at the prom,
Because I don't want to miss that dance,
I know you didn't mean to hurt,
I'm so sorry I got you wrong
I wasn't that alert,
Maybe if we could work things again,
One more kiss will make me forget this pain,
I know you're going through a lot,
I still have those pink tulips in my pot,
I know these days are scary for me and you,
But don't leave my hand and will get it through,
You're my hope in the dark,
Just like I'm your bird lark,

I know I pushed you aside,

But now every day is hell when you're not beside,

I know you've always been so caring,

But I'm so sorry for the misunderstanding,

Please come back and hold my hand,

I know now what I lost was a good friend,

I promise I won't create a bluff this time,

I want to hang out with you and have a bottle of wine,

I know it's not too late to apologize,

So I'm writing you this letter,

Cause this is not our closure,

I know I'm not better,

This is my apology to you in the form of a letter,

Please be here to make me feel better,

I know you would walk your footsteps back to my streets,

I'll be waiting for you, it doesn't matter if it takes weeks and weeks.

- Smruti Patel

38. Over the creeks

It's strange when everyone tells you what to do,
Where to walk and where not to go,
But I'm always surprised by the opinions I get,
Should I hold it or regret them,
The dorm is filled with butterflies and also with moths,
Should I take sunshine or walk in the forest filled with frost?
But I do the wise thing, unseeing these problems,
When I have a key to find all the solutions,
So I go and visit the library,
From where I pick a book,
I've got something to hold on to like a hook,
The old rusted books with that vintage smell,
Teaches me something important before I fell,
I read it till I relate it all to myself,
It's completely okay to look for a higher-shelf,
When I start flipping the pages,
It takes me back to the ages,
It feels like everything is fictional,
But the joy I get is irresistible,
Where I can be any character I want,
Peter or wendy,
Life here is more beautiful than disassembling yourself to be trendy,

I sit by the windows encircling myself with the fragranced candle,

A candle's light glows in the night as my silhouette dance with calm delight,

In the same way when flames grew with the heat on cue,

Every message I read always reminds me of you,

I read and read,

I repeat,

I read and read,

Till the last page tinges my fingertips,

Till every teardrop makes a small lake on the chevy table,

That is enough to sail a paper boat on it,

Till all my anger crystallizes

Till all the brokenness in me precipitates,

When the story brings back a smile to my lips,

And it all feels like I'm all over the creeks,

Reading never makes my bones feel weak,

Some anecdotes are so emotional that tears start rolling down my cheeks,

Reading books to me always feels like I'm all over the creeks,

I don't care about what he or she thinks,

Reading books makes me grope like I am all over the creeks.

-My experience stepping into the world of reading

- Smruti Patel

39. 15 seconds

When a vase gets broken, no one knows into how many pieces
it breaks,
When someone hurts you, you don't know how much
amount of tears your eyes leak,
When you put your body and soul into everything,
Still, you fail to pull off that string,
It's very easy to immobilize someone,
And even harder to patch again,
Cause you just spoke something mean,
Without caring about that person will they have someone's
side after you to lean?
It's lenient to create a mess,
And correspondingly so damn difficult to pick it up,
Because it only takes 15 seconds to burn things out, but
fifteen fucking more years to patch it again,
So think twice before you step inside the fire,
That might look like water to you, and then burns you deep
down,
And when it becomes hard to find yourself.

- Smruti Patel

40. Wisteria

It's white November,
I am waiting for July,
Colors start to droop,
That put me in white light,
I replay all my recollections,
Ambling down the roads,
How can I combat so many loads?
Try to find where all the flowers are lost,
That used to bloom the most,

Penning letters,
Just to feel better,
And I started scouring myself,
A book that I lowered down from my life shelf,
How can I be fine,
When there's nothing around me but the trees of pine,
Hey, April guess I'm feeling moistened,
Can't remember the paths that I'd walked,
I replay my footsteps on each stepping branch,
On the very branch all the flowers were gone,
Sniffing the essence to be so sworn,
Even though I tried my best to rehearse,
And then I started searching for myself,
Barefoot walking on cobblestones,
Getting bruised,
I had this feeling so worst,
Everything looked more like rust,
After days and days slipped,
Slowly and slowly,
The season takes a drift,
The coldness vanishes,
The tenderness shows up,
The flowers come back to joy,
They start showing their dances again,
When finally after enduring the burning sensation and
walking a long way,
My life begins,

Feels like I'm on the edge of the ridge,

And I got something to hold on to,

I see the worst feelings in me as they shed,

And now I've started blooming in red,

And see all the sun rays sneakin' in my bed,

After all the calamities,

Wisteria starts to camouflage,

I wonder how can it turn itself in these many tints and tones,

Someday white,

Someday purple,

Someday lilac,

I see the violet light that wisteria radiates,

That gives me faith to fight all threats,

I hush, and now there it's complete silence,

After all these rough days and violence,

And now I place myself,

Petals of wisteria healing my scars and back,

I see a dream of me better than ever,

This pain wouldn't saturate me forever,

And wisteria started to flourish in my life forevermore.

-The feeling when you defeat the darkness and let wisteria grow.

- Smruti Patel

41. When an Aquarius loves

Dear future lover,

Hi, it's me Aquarius, yeah, I know it sounds annoying,

I don't know who I'll be with but hope I'll be something to someone, someday,

But I assure you that you'll be the luckiest person on the whole planet cause you'll always be safe and sound with an Aquarius,

I'll love you with all your flaws,

I won't judge you for your weakness,

I would hold you even if the daylight pokes through your window,

But I would like honesty and love from your side,

Cause I'm done being broken every time,

I'll try my best to keep you entertained with my stupid talks,

I'll hold your hand in every walk that you'll walk,

Cause I think no one knows better than me the feeling of being alone,

Spend your day in the lonely corner of your room,

I'll write you some letters,

When things ain't working better,

I'll be misery in the dark if you try to break me,

I would expect nothing but support from your side,

But don't you dare try to hide things from me in the back of
my mind,
I'll take all your worries and make them mine,
I won't argue even if I have no reasons to shine,
Sometimes I also feel so broken but I don't express it,
But that doesn't mean you can blame me for everything,
Silence doesn't mean that you should always tolerate it even if
it's wrong,
I warn you, you better be strong,
I can write you so many songs whenever you'll feel low,
I swear it'll melt your heart slow,
I can play you some songs on guitar,
But don't expect that I like counting stars,
Because they are numerous and have their version of
themselves,
I would love you twice and thrice if you'll always gift me
fictional books to keep on our bookshelves,
Yeah, I may sound a little old school type,
But I'm kinda different from everyone else hype,
I won't tell you to become like me, I would always tell you
who you wanna be,
I'm great at writing monologues,
I'm obsessed with Taylor Swift and I can't stand any word if
it's against her,
Let's see where these lifeboats want me to go,
In the ocean or an old county road,
Regardless one thing no one will love you as an Aquarius does.

\- Smruti Patel

42. Looking back at you

You have a charming face but an awful heart,
You took my hand just so you could pull me apart,
Well stupid emotional naive little me, caught up in your feelings but now I see myself bleed,
If you would've been a little honest,
I might have played you a song,
I wish you would've treated me right I might have still loved you more,
I was so excited to write a song about you,
But the second moment you took all the butterflies that I had for you,
So it goes like if I would've known how to play the piano,
I might have written some songs about you,
but I'm thankful to myself,
that I didn't know how to play,
'cause you weren't strong to hold my lyrics what they wanna say,'
If I wrote a song about you it would be nothing but a waste of pages and hours,
It's good I am trying to forget about you,
I know it's hard but I need to do that soon,
I'm trying my best not to look back at you.

- Smruti Patel

43. 18

It's a narrative about
How fastly I turned 18,
Time slipped away like yesterday's flurry,
I feel it's cool to be a teen,
When you'll have one of those handsome boys to lean,
So I just opened all the doors,
And see as the daisies that bloom through my windows,
I have a scabrous way to walk till' I reach that far,
I was a trapped Beatle just waiting to be set free from a barbed
jar,
Then comes a phase called distraction,
He's so charming and I can't resist his reflection,
And I have something for him called affection,
But sadly he never knew,
The way I used to think about him,
Cause he is surrounded by so many diamonds,
How can someone see a Ruby-like me shining?
That is not that charming and the way I reflect is dim,
That broke me to the bone,
And I remain that untouched stone,
That someone would have never known,
Except for one, she's got my back,
And for me, nothing's lacking,

A friend, a place, a guitar,

To hang over all the murkiness of the nights,

And they never give me an awful fright,

To me, they are sunrays of my darkest days,

Then came a phase when I sensed I was criticized,

As I walk past the pave,

I felt they might end me to the grave,

They assume I was too young,

I think they've just got me wrong,

As soon as I heard those words,

It shattered all my wings,

That was just preparing to fly,

I lost my arcade ring,

Even though I tried,

I fell hard,

Well, that sounds absurd,

But for me, it sounds cool to lurk,

When you have a good friend to snuck,

You'll miss this joy when you'll grow hoary,

You'll be a faded curtain and start lying on the ground like a torn and worn tapestry,

It's completely normal if you hate chemistry,

Sometimes I saw that,

All my friends weren't the ones who I thought,

So I decided I don't want such people to be around me when I'm clean,

When they'll be the reason to dust on me when I'll try to glow,

All I do is light a lamp in my room,

I watch all those tuberoses on my front porch as they blossom,

They always gleam and gloom,

Despite the dust and snow,

Then came a firefly flying through my window,

It taught me,

Enjoy every moment like a willow,

Before you turn completely hollow,

Just go with the winds,

Left to right,

Don't bother if it's day or midnight,

So I light a candle to my soul,

I'm no more scared of any of these rabbit holes,

I'll reach the sky if I try,

My faith in me healed all my wounds,

The next decade I came up flying with my patched wings,

Stop wasting your precious time on all these reckless things,

I told myself I'm ready to think,

And wink,

And it's not easy,

Roads that we walk sometimes may turn dizzy,

I learned a lesson,

Nothing's more important than your passion,

I had a rollercoaster for a while,

Running in my mind,

That is all I felt as I turned 18,

I realized it isn't that cool to be a teen,

I'd rather choose to be older and wise,

And I'm still trying to figure out to fill my void,

And thank you,

18,

For making me realize.

- Smruti Patel

44. The best place

There are a lot of places to go,

But you exactly know a place where to go when you're upset,

You can share your feelings with your best friend watching the sunset,

Starting right from school,

To be friends forever,

The journey you had was so interesting,

Can't put it in the picture frame or scribble it somewhere,

Except to play that vibe in your heart,

Late-night talks on the cell phone sneaking into your blanket,

Afraid if someone catches you,

But that's the phase from where you learn to take risks,

When you have a tightrope to hold on to and lean on,

You can easily make-out looking at your Bffs' eyes that she's upset,

Then you do something absurd to bring that smile back,

Someday you'll grow older and try to travel a lot of places,

But you'll always miss those tip-toeing on that streets, heading for home together after school,

Sometimes auburn looks more beautiful than pastel colors,

Sometimes not telling anything speaks a lot,

When you recall that walks and talks it brings a grin to your face,

When you recall each debate and argument or reminds you of
your childish aspect,
But you've grown now,
Then try to apologize for your blunders by writing an apology
letter,
And make things better,
It's more than something but can't say,
It's less than something it kinda maims,
I might not sound overwhelming,
It is the same old me,
I'm not good with confessing,
But I try to express it invisibly, the same warmth, care,
concern,
It's amazing to know that the same person likes you today,
I think I'm a little old-school type,
But I like it that way,
I love tea when it burns on that slow flame,
Everything looks good when it's slow,
But you are the best place that I know.

- Smruti Patel

45. Blue

Lavender girls in acrylic vases,
Perfect lips and perfect bodies,
They all belong in vintage magazines,
Those fancy girls the boys are dating,
They're always playing their ace,
Hanging around with those handsome faces,
Wishing you would see me waiting there,
Hoping you were with me,
But I'm blue a little dizzy,
If I were a violet, maybe you'd
love me,
But remember this blue is always there for you...
Paris beauty in beautiful palaces,
Perfect eyes with perfect dresses,
They all belong to that royal places,
Those queens the kings are kissing,
Hanging around with those handsome faces,
Wishing you would see me,
But I'm blue, not that pretty,
I were a red maybe you'd picked me,
But remember this blue is always there for you,
Pretty girls in dark places,
broken hearts like broken vases,

Flowers like me strewn in grasses,
Don't forget about me soon,
This blue is always there for you,

• 115 •

-just love the way you are, cause you know how unique you
are don't change into someone to be with someone, be happy
with who you are, be the blue in dark.

- Smruti Patel

—

How can I love someone else,
When I'm too weary to accept who I am,
How can I make someone feel what it's like to be loved,
When I've never even felt any of it,
All I felt till now is to be alone,
Guess I'm tip toeing back home,
I'm driving back home, at least those Curtains in my room don't
make me feel alone,
I'm driving back home,
cause I'm fine playing guitar sitting by the windows, at least
playing a song doesn't make me feel hollow... I'm driving back
home.

\- Smruti Patel

Every kiss that you gave me now seems like a scar,
you made me believe in daydreams, but honestly now I hate
counting all the stars, we both leave nearby still we're way too far,
it took you five minutes to break up on the phone, and tear us
apart,
down came the snow, storming, and thunder,

I thought we would walk the pavement,
but there's nothing left in me to wonder.

- Smruti Patel

If you meant when you said you loved me then where did you get
the nerve to drop my hand if you wanted to leave me you
should've taught me how to live with a broken heart, you
should've taught me how to try not to think about you, you
should've taught me how to dance alone under the street lights,
you should've taught me how to live with a broken heart.

- Smruti Patel

The way his eyes looked into mine when he first saw me waiting
by the lockers,
For the first time in my life, I saw,
Shades of hue and wine,
I can still see them shine the same, but now the difference is they
never stare into mine as they used to.

- Smruti Patel

I'm a little faded, but I have a little shine,

You like pastel colors, but I like Auburn,

I like driving in the car, and you like counting stars,

I'm a little scared of losing everything cause nothing belongs to

me,

you have everything but still,

you don't wanna see,

oh, you should try to put yourself in my place then you'd know,

what it's like to be spending the past few months alone,

how could you ever feel what it's like to feel that way, but imma

tell you,

feel so hurt when no one wants to know you better, yeah it hurts

when no one wants to let you in,

it hurts a lot when no one wants to know you anymore, days are

sunny but for me,

it's getting darker when no one wants me anymore.

- Smruti Patel

Looking back at you,
you used to look so good, looking at me right now,
haven't figured out since you left me this time,
So tell me, did you have to leave so soon, I'm sitting by the
windows in the quiet of the night,
Dancing alone under the pale moonlight, Back when you and I
were two walls in the same room,
Now you and I are a complete disaster, two different ways never
meant where they wanted to go,
And I'm vacant since you said goodbye...
It's so sad you'll never love me then,
And I'm feeling like sinking ever since you said goodbye.

- Smruti Patel

I'm feeling jealous,
By seeing her kiss you,
I'm feeling horrible,
Man that girl for you is a big trouble
Anyway, you'll never get what I want to say,
She ain't worth you anyway,

She's just not like what you think,

I'm here to warn you before you shrink,

Then don't come crying that I didn't offer you a hint,

This won't work out for you, soon it'll start to stain,

You might now feel I sound mean,

I'm the best advice on which you can learn,

She only likes you cause you're handsome,

She won't hold you for Ransome,

The last thing is you don't see, I love you for so many reasons,

I don't care whether it's any season,

I can tell what's wrong with you staring into your eyes,

I can see day by day your turning blind,

She's pretty but not kind,

She doesn't know how to read your mind,

She never loves you like the way I do,

Because she only loves you for your looks,

That's what I can see sneaking behind my book,

Why don't you see it, She only loves you for your looks.

- Smruti Patel

You should've been a shrewd man,

Instead of being so fucking mean,

You should've kissed me once
Before you let me leave,
Now I don't know?
What am I gonna do?
Where am I gonna go?
How am I gonna heal?
Is there someone to hear any more about the way I feel,
Do you even feel fine,
After burning the things that used to shine,
I keep pretending to others that I'm fine,
So, you should've just kept me then let go,
Now it's raining instead of snow,
What was coming how am I supposed to know,
Now it's raining instead of snow.

- Smruti Patel

She broke her promise that she made to me, that she'll take me to
Coney Island by this weekend, she came back home and said
honey we won't be able to hang out today, tears started rolling
down my cheeks, I felt bad she broke the promise she made, she
worked day and night to make the company gain it's weight few
years after when I grew up I discern that she worked hard for me,

to give me all the comfort that she can so that she can spend her
penny on my petty dreams, our minds are so mean that sometimes
we don't see that our mom's do everything unconditionally, they
say the truth that we'll never grow up.

- Smruti Patel

I solved every puzzle that was sneakin' in your heart, but you
weren't wise enough and now that it hurts, I'm the one lurking,
I'm the one lingering for you, how you did make me believe in
fairytales and the second moment you took the smile that we use
to fake, there are so many polaroids of you, hanging in my room, I
comb through our memories when I see it through, if you were
wise enough, we might have been together, I tried to remove the
dagger, how can a person be so nice, one moment good the other
way never wise, all I think is do you even think of me, I wish if
you would see what you didn't see, you would've never been so
mean, I wish to be with you if you were me.

- Smruti Patel

How easily I was caught up by the moment that I almost sensed
that he smells like a rose to me, but when I tried to wrap myself

around him I realized it felt more like a thorn, I think it's so easy
to mess up with your feelings when you become so blind for
someone else's attention that you don't feel the stings that hurt you
because you find the smell and red color on the roses but you can't
feel the pain that it gives you when you try to make it yours or try
to hold on it.

- Smruti Patel

I can hear that jazz record that you are playing in your apartment,
even though I live feet apart from you, can't help but your gravity
is pulling me a little bit closer, what do you think, the boy should
I write you a letter or a closure, everything is slipping out of my
hand I'm dancing on those jazz beats even if I hate, look what are
you doing to me now even if you have done nothing to me till
now, what will happen next I don't know somehow.

- Smruti Patel

New day, but same old you, Want to step out but how could you,
cause you've never been to the outside, you wanna run out see the
world, but nobody lets you in, cause nobody lets me in, I dreamed
for a life with a bunch of good friends, here I'm am in my room
drunk on my feelings, is there someone beside me to heal it?, no
one cares what I'm feeling...

The best thing you can do is self-sabotage, and happiness Is just
being who you are, cause I think I was never meant to walk
outside, so I prefer to stay inside, it's all me alone at the end of the
day..

- Smruti Patel

Last night you showed up at my place, with a bottle of vintage
wine, we drank a lot of it, didn't realize when we got into the fight,
maybe unknowingly, or was it real I saw a side of you which I wish
I would've never seen, that's the reason I'm scared of vintage wine,
I thought I could hold you forever but now you gave me no
reasons to call you mine.

- Smruti Patel

About the Author

Smruti is the kind of person who looks for inspiration for writing in every possible way. She's mostly busy writing songs and poems, often scribbling it in the back of her notebook in college. She's a die-hard fan of Taylor Swift and country music. Writing is her forever escapism that doesn't make her feel forlorn.
Writing to her means everything, she completely jams with good music and Hollywood movies. She loves being aesthetic, she loves to maintain a journal too.
She just loves herself the way she is.